TO MAUREEN.

LOVE FROM LESLIE

DEC '08.

a gift of
inner peace

a gift of
inner peace

Gill Farrer-Halls
With illustrations from the
collection of Robert Beer

MQP

Published by MQ Publications Limited
12 The Ivories, 6–8 Northampton Street
London, N1 2HY
Tel: 020 7359 2244
Fax: 020 7359 1616
Email: mail@mqpublications.com
Website: www.mqpublications.com

Copyright © MQ Publications Limited 2003
Text © Gill Farrer-Halls 2003
Illustrations © Robert Beer 2003

Series editor: Abi Rowsell
Design: Yvonne Dedman

ISBN: 1 84072 395 5

1 3 5 7 9 0 8 6 4 2

contents

introduction   7

karma path to inner peace   33

kindness   65

letting go   91

a good life   121

faith   153

impermanence and change   179

regret and resolve   207

patience   231

about the artist   254

acknowledgments   256

introduction

The Sanskrit word *karma* is now part of the English language. Expressions such as "bad karma" and "good karma" are commonly used these days. Jokes such as "Your karma ran over my dogma" are amusing but don't make sense, and expose the fact that most of us native English speakers do not have much understanding of the true meaning of the word. We tend to use this term to describe a sort of mystical fate or fortune, which is not entirely incorrect but does miss the full meaning and subtle complexities of what karma is and how it works in our lives. This book takes a look at what karma really means.

Firstly, note that the original texts of Buddhism were written in Sanskrit and Pali. Karma is called "kamma" in Pali, the Indic language used in the canonical books of Buddhism. You will see both versions in the quotations used in this book, but they mean the same thing.

The law of karma

Sometimes people refer to the law of karma as a natural and inescapable law of the universe. While integral to Buddhist teachings, including those about compassion and wisdom, essentially karma means action, although this is a general definition.

More precisely, Buddhists say that karma refers to actions that are willed or meant—that is, those that have intention behind them. However, even if we do something instinctively, without thinking about it, there is still some level of unconscious intention at work.

Therefore, all of our actions can create karma. Their effects can vary between being powerful or weak depending on different conditions and situations. Traditional Buddhist texts state that Buddhas, or people who have become enlightened, are the only ones whose actions are perfectly "pure" and which no longer generate karma.

Mental, verbal, and bodily karma

Karma has a threefold classification:

1. mental karma—created by the mind and thoughts,
2. verbal karma—created by speech, and
3. bodily karma—caused by physical actions.

Mental karma is the most significant of the three because it gives rise to, and is the origin of, the other two types of karma. We think before we speak or physically do something, however briefly, and our thoughts influence what we say and do.

Furthermore, two types of karmic actions are described here: ones that are positive, skillful, beneficial, and also good, and those that are negative, unskillful, harmful, and ultimately bad.

Ten negative actions that create bad karma

There are ten main negative actions that create bad karma: the three physical acts of killing, stealing, and sexual misconduct (including acts such as adultery); followed by the four negative acts of speech, i.e., lying, saying things to harm others or cause conflict between them, using harsh language such as swearing, and idle gossip; and ending with the three mental negative acts of covetousness, thinking ill of people, and holding wrong views, such as not understanding that anger causes suffering.

Ten positive actions that create good karma

These involve, first, giving up all negative actions, as noted before, and then cultivating their positive opposites. The three physical virtues are protecting life, being generous to others, and responsible sexual behavior. The four positive acts of speech include being truthful, creating harmony and reconciliation among others, talking pleasantly, and having useful conversations. The three mental virtues are being content with what one has, being kind to others, and developing conviction that what the Buddha taught is beneficial.

Negative karma

Negative karma arises from actions that are driven by ignorance or delusion; hatred, aversion, or anger; or greed, attachment, or avarice. These are called the Three Poisons in Buddhism, and are the qualities that keep us trapped in samsara, the cycle of birth and rebirth, which we only escape by reaching enlightenment.

Positive karma

Positive karma arises from actions that are not rooted in ignorance, hatred, or greed. Although we could say positive karma arises from wisdom, love, and renunciation, it is traditional to describe the positive qualities as directly opposite to the Three Poisons, because this reminds us of what they are and to try to avoid them.

Three stages must occur for an action to be complete:

1. the motivation to perform the action,
2. the successful fulfillment of the action, and
3. the satisfaction of completing the action.

If only one or two stages are fulfilled, the karma created is less, while a completed action generates greater karmic consequences. For example, if you mistakenly squash an insect and are sorry to have killed it, only the action itself has occurred; there was no intention or satisfaction in the act.

The karmic consequences are, therefore, less than if you deliberately jumped on the insect and were happy to have successfully killed it.

The law of cause and effect

Karma is also called the law of cause and effect. This means that every action, however tiny or seemingly insignificant, creates a cause for an eventual result, which is called the fruit of the action. These consequences are complex and influenced by hundreds of little factors during our lives, and through many different lifetimes, that intermingle. Because of this, we often cannot see clearly how karma operates.

Karmic fruition may be
experienced in this lifetime,
in the next lifetime,
or in other, future lives.

Karmic fruition

Most human actions create karmic consequences that are not experienced immediately but will definitely be experienced later.

The Buddhist scriptures say that the majority of our actions will bear fruit in future lives. A kind, generous, honest person who suffers in this life can rest assured he or she will experience the positive karmic consequences of his or her good actions in a later life. Someone behaving in ways that cause suffering for others, but enjoying a happy life, will suffer the consequences of the negative behavior in a later life.

Karma and rebirth

Karma and rebirth are deeply interlinked. What exactly is rebirth? Buddhism considers that only our most subtle consciousness goes from one life to the next. The individual person, both personality and characteristics, is extinguished at death. This subtle consciousness carries with it all the karma created in the life just finished, together with any karma from previous lives that has not yet come to fruition. These karmic imprints determine the quality of the next life, while some of the karma carried over will also come to fruition in the next life when it meets the appropriate conditions.

Certain behavior creates specific karmic consequences

A person who easily finds prosperity in this life may have created the cause by being generous in a previous existence. Someone who dies young in this life might have failed to protect others in a previous life.

Beauty could be the result of pure ethical behavior in a past life, while people who are not taken seriously in this life may have created the cause by lying in a past existence. These examples illustrate how karma is linked with ethical, responsible behavior—we reap what we sow.

Black and white

Karma is classified according to its results. The first category is called

- **black** karma, **black** result

and includes all harmful actions of body, speech, and mind.

- white karma, white result

incorporates all nonharmful and virtuous actions.

- **black** and white karma,
  black and white result

includes actions that are partly harmful, partly not. For example, telling a lie in order not to hurt someone's feelings. Although the intention is positive, the act itself is not, so the karmic consequences will be mixed.

The last category needs more explanation. This is:

- karma that is neither **black** nor white,
  a result that is neither **black** nor white.

This arises when our underlying intention is to transcend the other kinds of karma altogether by trying to become enlightened, the ultimate goal of Buddhism. The purpose of practicing Buddhism is to avoid suffering and find happiness. This may make us feel that creating karma that brings happiness as the result is the best thing to do.

However, Buddhism teaches us that everything is impermanent, so even if we create the causes of happiness, the resulting happiness cannot last forever. Sooner or later the karma that created happiness will be exhausted and we will experience suffering. Our highest aspiration is to transcend karma on our path toward enlightenment.

Rebirth

While some early Christian sects believed in a form of rebirth, it is quite a difficult concept for some Westerners to accommodate. Since people are born with certain talents, however, we can begin to understand how karma moves from one life to the next. People with outstanding musical talent, for example, often speak of how they felt as if they already knew how to play music when they first started. Similarly, Mozart learned how to play music very quickly at an early age and had an inner sense of harmony and rhythm.

The Noble Eightfold Path

Attaining enlightenment is not easy! It is a state in which one is completely free from desire for, and attachment to, things one likes, and also from aversion to, and hatred for, what one doesn't like.

To develop the conditions within which this state may arise, Buddhists follow the Buddha's Noble Eightfold Path, which is a guide to living in a manner that does not cause suffering to oneself or others. It was created to help people reach enlightenment.

Enlightenment is the total liberation from suffering that the Buddha discovered, also referred to as nirvana and awakening.

This explanation of karma makes one thing very clear:

we are responsible for
whatever occurs in our lives.

The Noble Eightfold Path

The Noble Eightfold Path comprises:
1. Right view
2. Right thought
3. Right speech
4. Right action
5. Right livelihood
6. Right effort
7. Right mindfulness
8. Right concentration

The person who has happiness, health, and success created the foundations for a pleasant life by performing positive actions in previous lives.

Those who suffer illness, poverty, and so forth, likewise created the causes for their unpleasant experiences by committing negative actions previously. Most people have a mixture of good and bad experiences throughout their lives, reflecting the varied karma they created in earlier lives. So, karma is not fatalistic. By consciously trying to act with wisdom, love, kindness, and compassion for others as much as possible, we create the karma for positive rebirths. Virtuous behavior will eventually lead us beyond karma altogether, to enlightenment.

Purification

So, can anything be done about all the negative karma that has been created over many different lifetimes? Obviously it would be preferable not to experience all the bad karmic results! There is a way to erase some of our negative karma—purification. This requires understanding that you have behaved badly in the past and that you must take full responsibility for this behavior. Then you must sincerely regret and repent your negative actions and promise yourself to try not to behave badly again. Finally, try to perform only positive, virtuous actions from now on.

Just as musical talent may be the karmic result of musical training in an earlier life, behavioral patterns can also be karmic results. For example, if someone gets angry easily, this may be seen as a karmic consequence of previous angry behavior that the person now has the opportunity to purify. The person needs to try hard not to give in to the impulse to be angry, by reflecting that anger will create more negative karma and further intensify the habit of growing angry. While not easy, this is definitely worth attempting in order to avoid harming oneself and others in the present and in future lives.

That is a very brief introduction to karma. The following chapters examine in greater depth how karma operates and affects our lives. Practical suggestions and advice on how to generate good karma and avoid bad karma, will be offered, along with some inspiring quotations.

Once the profound nature
of karma is properly understood,
a path that can lead
to a happier life
may be discovered.

karma path to
inner peace

I nner peace is the quiet, untroubled, spacious quality of mind that we all yearn for but rarely find in daily life. To some extent, this lack of peace and quiet reflects our modern culture, where time has become a precious commodity.

Do you find that you never seem to have enough time, and you generally spend your life rushing between work, home, and social activities? By the time you fall into bed each night, you probably feel not only exhausted, but full of stress from living this lifestyle. How can you use the concept of karma to improve your life,

THE MAHASIDDHA NIRGUNA

Nirguna, the "man without qualities," was one of the eighty-four Indian Mahasiddha. He is depicted here seated in the posture of "royal ease."

and, going beyond a hectic daily schedule, find this elusive sense of inner peace?

As noted in the introduction to this book, one basic definition of karma is the law of cause and effect. You can use the idea of cause and effect to examine how you live your life, and whether you can initiate any changes to improve your situation. Of course there is much about life that seems inevitable, such as the need to have some kind of work to pay for your way through life. For most of us, giving up everything and going to live in a country retreat or on a tropical island is an impossible thing to contemplate. However, giving up some things may be useful and will help you to reflect upon what brings you happiness in your life and what causes you dissatisfaction; such reflection will also enable you to decide what it is you would like to abandon on your quest to find inner peace.

Managing work and relaxation

For most people, more time is spent at work than in any other activity. If you are lucky, you enjoy your job, but almost everyone finds work tiring and difficult at times. This then creates a desire to compensate yourself as much as possible when you

are not working or asleep. If you enjoy yourself by spending your hard-earned money in an endless pursuit of sensory gratification, it will create a karmic cycle of work and material consumption that is self-perpetuating: one activity feeding the other. This leaves little time to experience peace and quiet.

So what can you do to make the time you spend at work less unpleasant and more enjoyable?

First, examine your working situation. Perhaps it would be possible to change your job to some other way of making a living that you would find

THE MAHASIDDHA TANTIPA

Tantipa was an old weaver who attained enlightenment while practicing at his loom.

more rewarding, even if it meant earning a little less money. Job satisfaction is more life-affirming than being wealthy but unhappy. Most people need to do some lateral, creative thinking about this. Even if you cannot change the kind of work you do, or your actual job, you can at least change your attitude about it. For instance, instead of indulging negative feelings about work, you can accept your situation and not fight against it.

Understanding that your aversion to work only causes you personal suffering and does not change anything will help you find ways to make your time at work more enjoyable.

Happiness is to be found inside yourself—in your mind and feelings. Feeling calm and comfortable with yourself and your situation in life is the best foundation for happiness. External objects only provide temporary gratification. Often people can confuse the short-lived thrill of buying brand new objects with happiness. But such objects never make you happy for very long. No sooner do you buy the new dress or the new stereo than you immediately start craving something else. This is not happiness; this is desire. Remaining endlessly caught up in desire does not bring the inner peace and satisfaction that people long for.

Desire is a distraction

The society we live in encourages consumerism. It feeds desire through advertising, and advocates a materialistic lifestyle that only leads to debt and suffering. There is no harm in having nice possessions, but if you do not examine the karmic cause and effect of desire, you will never find inner peace. Desire often functions to distract you from underlying feelings of anxiety and existential fears. You may feel concerned about the meaning of life and what the purpose of your life is, but because these thoughts are disquieting, you opt for "retail therapy" to distract yourself from them.

If you want to find inner peace, you need to understand what its causes are, what actions and attitudes you need to take up or let go in order to find it. You may need to make changes in your life, although these need not be radical or difficult.

Try to create some time just for yourself, and use it to be quiet, and not do anything. You may notice that usually you are trapped in a karmic cycle of endless activity; if you are not at work, you are in a restaurant or a sports or night club, or slumped in front of the television.

How much time do you create in your life simply to do nothing, simply to be? We call ourselves

human beings, but spend most of our lives doing, not being.

This precious human life

The Buddhist texts state that it is fortunate for us to have a human life, as it is a rare opportunity to follow the path through to enlightenment. So Buddhists call it "this precious human life." Animals have limited minds and often act from compulsion, therefore creating endless negative karma, whereas humans can act from compassion and wisdom and create positive karma.

GREEN TARA

Detail of a painting of Green Tara showing some of the animal supports of her throne—elephant, lion, and mythical unicorn (sarabha).

Meditation

The practice of Buddhism introduces a wonderful method to make the most of the quiet time and space that determined people can carve out of their lives: this is known as meditation. Many people have found meditation to be beneficial for health, happiness, and inner peace.

Meditating regularly for ten to twenty minutes every day can help you discover real peace within yourself. It enables you to find happiness in just being alive. Being peaceful and happy creates good karma, because you are not driven by desire and aversion.

Meditation 1

To start meditating, all you need is the will to try it out for ten minutes and a quiet, private space. Follow these steps to discover how to meditate.

1 Sit comfortably and quietly on a chair, and observe your breathing. The sensations of breathing put you in touch with what it means to be alive; simply, if you don't breathe, you die. Sitting and watching your breathing makes you conscious of the wonder and preciousness of your life. It makes you aware of the present moment, the here and now.

2 Sit still with your back straight, head upright, both feet flat on the floor, your shoulders and upper arms relaxed, with your hands resting on your knees. Be relaxed, but not slumped.

3 Keep your eyes closed, or slightly open and focused on the floor a few feet in front of you.

4 Now bring your attention to your breathing. Notice how it feels when the air enters and leaves your nostrils. Just sitting and observing your breathing will help to ground you in the present moment.

5 You may find that you have stopped watching your breathing and your mind has wandered off into thoughts, daydreams, and fantasies. This is just a natural habit that takes time to change. If you find you get caught up in thinking rather than noticing your breath, gently return your attention to your breathing. Gradually your mind may become tranquil, and when you finish meditating you will feel rested and refreshed.

The wonder of meditation is that, over time and with lots of practice, you gradually learn not to follow all of your thoughts.

You will start to look at them as "just thoughts" that randomly pop into your mind, and you will realize you do not have to follow every thought that appears. For instance, you can just drop, or stop thinking about, disturbing or upsetting trains of thought. They are no more substantial than clouds passing across the sky. If you are lucky, you will become aware of the gaps between thoughts, moments of pure consciousness, and you will be able to discover the true, spacious nature of the mind, which is like a cloudless sky.

Other less structured, more informal ways to meditate include taking a walk somewhere quiet and beautiful. When you find peace and quiet inside yourself, you notice more of the little details that make up each moment of life; for example, how the wind rustles the leaves of the trees, or a sudden burst of birdsong.

Your bath time is an ideal opportunity to find inner peace by allowing you to tune in to the calm environment. Instead of playing music, or rushing through bathing quickly because you want to do something else, lie back and enjoy the warm water. Find deep relaxation by just quietly watching your breath come and go, enjoying the peace of the present moments.

Considered actions

There are other, less tranquil situations that you can use to transform anger and impatience into inner peace, instead of just mindlessly reacting to difficult circumstances. Perhaps you habitually become impatient waiting for a bus, and your usual response is to become increasingly agitated and worried about being late.

Looking at how karma operates in these situations can help to change stressful reactions, which only cause suffering and cannot alter circumstances. If you accept that the situation is

THE MAHASIDDHA LAKSMINKARA

Laksminkara, the mad princess, was one of the female Mahasiddhas of India. She is shown here dancing in a fiery charnel ground.

beyond your control, and that it is not your fault that the journey might make you late, then you can begin to relax. If you remain stressed and angry, you will only cause further suffering to yourself and others.

Changing your reactions and feelings is not an easy process to go through. These are conditioned mental, and emotional, karmic habits that have managed to accumulate over this life and previous lifetimes. Therefore, you cannot force these changes; they need to arise naturally as a result of your decision to change.

SARASVATI'S SWAN

Detail of a painting of Sarasvati, the goddess of knowledge and the arts. The swan is her vehicle or mount, and holds a lotus bud in its beak as an offering.

In order to counteract and alleviate the irritation and frustration that arises from being late, you should pay attention to your breathing. When you are angry and impatient, your breathing becomes quick and shallow, which in turn causes other physiological reactions in your body.

Some of these reactions are referred to as the "fight or flight" syndrome. Making yourself breathe deeply and slowly calms you down mentally as well as physically.

Now that you feel calmer, look at the cause and the effect of the situation. Has anything in your

ROCKS AND WATER

Detail of a painting of a Bodhisattva, showing rock formations, water, and clouds.

behavior caused the situation, such as missing the early train and having to take the next one? If anything you have done has contributed to the cause, you need to accept it. If you feel that circumstances have conspired against you, and you haven't done anything to cause the lateness, then you must accept that too. Next, look at your feelings and emotions themselves.

Impatience, anger, frustration, and irritation—all of these feelings are making you feel pain and suffering. Recognizing that you do not want to suffer is an important step toward eliminating suffering in your life.

A measured approach

By looking long and hard at your negative feelings and recognizing that they only cause you suffering, you can change them. You can reflect upon past occasions when you had negative feelings. Perhaps you were feeling so angry by the time you arrived late at work that you ended up in an argument with someone, which continued your suffering and made someone else suffer too.

Remembering this will help you realize how your negative feelings are pointless and damaging, and this may then help the feelings start to lessen. You can reflect that, in the whole vastness of your life, one little, isolated incident of being late for something is quite insignificant. In a couple of days the chances are you won't even remember it. Seeing the situation in this way helps you transform your anger into a calmer state.

If you follow some of the suggestions in this book, you will gradually start to feel calmer and more peaceful. The calming practice of meditation allows you to feel more content with what you have in life, so that you do not fall prey to continual desire and craving. It also helps you accept the unpleasant things in life without reacting so badly to them.

Looking at the effect of negative emotions on yourself and others also helps you let them go and regain inner peace. By contemplating and analyzing the nature of negative emotions you gradually come to the understanding that they only bring suffering. For example, when you feel great attachment to some object or person, recall a previous attachment to a similar person or object. Reflect that although at the time the object seemed so precious, now something else has replaced it. Coming to an understanding that the objects of attachment are impermanent will bring peace of mind.

Understanding karma
allows you to take responsibility
for creating your own happiness,
and you eventually discover
the inner peace and contentment
you only used to dream of.

LAMA CHODPA MANDALA

Mandala of the Five Buddhas with Vajradhara at the center.

Kindness

Karma is a complex subject, and can be a bit frightening when you first start thinking about it. Once you understand that all of your actions shape your future, you might begin to feel intimidated about the full extent of the implications of karma.

However, one thing you can remember easily is kindness. Trying to be kind to others as much as possible in day-to-day life is a beneficial way to transform your negative behavior. Simple acts of kindness to others and yourself can create positive karma in your life and help you to find inner peace and calm.

My religion is kindness.

The Dalai Lama

What exactly is kindness? You need to be careful not to patronize others in the act. If you think, "Oh, I'm being so kind to this poor person—that must make me a really good person," this is not true kindness. On the other hand, if you develop empathy with others as much as possible, and really try to understand their feelings and needs, then you can respond with love and true kindness in appropriate ways.

Kind is my love today,
tomorrow kind,
Still constant
in a wondrous excellence.

William Shakespeare

GREEN TARA

Detail of a miniature painting of Green Tara, showing her left
hand in the gesture of protection or giving refuge as she holds
the stem of a blue lotus flower.

Being kind is not always simple. For example, if someone asks us to help them hurt another person, such as enlisting our help to play a nasty practical joke on someone, then how should we respond? In a case like this, withholding our help and explaining why is the kindest thing we can do for that person.

In ancient India, certain monks used to walk everywhere slowly, carefully sweeping the path in front of them with a soft brush so as not to hurt any insects. Using this inspiring example, think of ways in your own life to be kind to animals.

GANAPATI (GANESH)

Detail of a copy of an early Nepali painting of Ganapati, showing the head of the rat upon which he stands, and the donor who commissioned this painting.

Being kind to others
creates the causes for each of us
to receive kindness from others.

Act from kindness

Kindness is as much a state of mind, or attitude, as the act itself. If you are kind to someone but with a hard heart and through gritted teeth, this is not real kindness, and so the karmic consequences of your action will be mixed.

You cannot expect to like everyone you meet. However, you can at least refrain from being unkind to those you don't like. This is an indirect form of kindness.

Kindness is an art

Be aware of your personal limits, as you are not a bottomless well of kindness. Be realistic about your own ability. Learn when it is a good time to respond with kindness and when it would actually be too much for you to cope with. Otherwise, when you feel the intention to be kind, but do not succeed for some reason out of your control, you will feel disappointed and angry with yourself for failing.

The purpose of dharma
(Buddhist teachings)
is to help our mind
to expand, to grow, to clarify.
It should uphold us and create
an inner sense of
peace, joy, and clarity.

Tenzin Palmo

THE YANTRAS OF SIXTEEN HINDU DEITIES

The Hindu Yantra or "device" is similar in form to the Buddhist
mandala, and consists of interlocking triangles in a lotus circle
within a palace with four gateways.

Kindness is an art. It is possible for you to be creative in the ways you express kindness to others if you really think about it. If you use your imagination, being kind to others can be fun as well as personally rewarding.

An act of kindness can take only a few seconds, like holding a door open for an overloaded shopper. But experiencing a kind act like this can make someone happy all day.

Meditation 11

Here's a basic ten-minute meditation on kindness for you to practice.

1 Sit quietly with a straight back and observe your breathing for a few moments.

2 Reflect on the innumerable kind acts people have shown you, such as your mother looking after you when you were a baby. According to Buddhism, because we have innumerable lives, everyone at some point has been your mother.

3 Think about how you would like to repay everyone for their kindness toward you.

4 Develop your motivation to be kind to everyone, and feel happy that you will have opportunities to be kind to others in this life.

The various features and aspects
of human life,
such as longevity, good health,
success, happiness, and so forth,
which we consider desirable,
are all dependent on kindness
and a good heart.

The Dalai Lama

LOTUS AND AURA

Detail of a red lotus blossoming at the edge of a Bodhisattva's aura.

A smile can brighten
someone's day;
a scowl can darken
someone's dreams.

It is incredibly easy to be kind to a nice person, and very hard to be kind to a mean person. But the mean person is the one who is suffering most, and therefore is most in need of kindness. So it is important to try extra hard to be kind to people who are unkind, and this will help them change their negative behavior.

The more you practice kindness instead of selfishness, the more you will become accustomed to behaving in a kind manner. Then eventually your kindness becomes spontaneous, and you will no longer think that you must act kindly. You simply feel kind toward others from the bottom of your heart. This is pure kindness.

When you feel angry and want to direct it at someone as a way of expressing your anger, try to take yourself out of the situation and find solitude until your anger has passed. This is a skillful way of not being unkind to anyone, which is in itself an indirect form of kindness.

When people around us are suffering, we
should be sensitive and compassionate and help
them to the best of our ability. But we should
not get so involved that their problem becomes our
problem and we become tense and worried over it.
We can avoid this by recalling that the cause
and the solution of any problem lie in the mind
of the person experiencing it . . . As long as we are
loving and kind and do whatever we can to
ease their pain, we should not feel guilty or
inadequate and think we must do more.

Kathleen McDonald

PADMASAMBHAVA

Detail of Padmasambhava's left hand, holding a skull-cup full of
immortal nectar and a golden flask. He wears three distinct layers
of clothing, all of which are embroidered with golden designs.

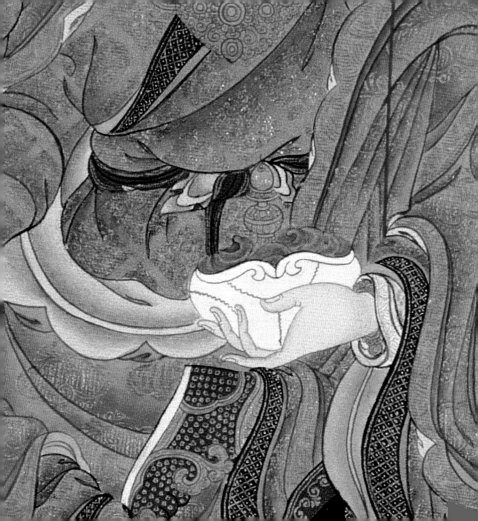

Even if we are materially poor,
we can still offer
the gift of kindness.

Mindful kindness

Be mindful not to smother others with kindness. If someone is angry or depressed, you can ask how you can help, but often there is nothing else you can do. Sometimes the kindest act is to give people time and space for their feelings to change, and then see how you can help afterward.

PADMAPANI AVALOKITESHVARA

Detail of white Padmapani, the "lotus-handed" Bodhisattva of compassion, showing his right hand receiving an offering of three jewel-fruits from a crane.

A great Buddhist teacher once said that when you bang your knee, your hand immediately reaches out to rub it better. If we regard everyone similarly to ourselves, we can reach out to others spontaneously with kindness, in the same way that we instantly rub our painful knee. You can practice being kind so often that it becomes an automatic reaction without thought; you simply reach out as if it were yourself who were suffering.

Practice being kind to yourself, the better to be kind to others. When you feel like being unkind to someone, think first. It's not worth it, as it will eventually result in receiving unkindness yourself.

Less is more

Sometimes we don't feel as if we have much kindness to offer others, especially when we are suffering in some way. But even when you feel bad, you can still be polite and courteous to others, remembering to say thank you, and so forth. These little acts of kindness can actually help you feel better, as people often respond immediately with kindness in return. This creates a sense of kinship with others, so that you don't feel so alone, which will often improve your mood.

A kind person has many friends. We don't have to be clever or sophisticated to be kind. In fact, we

need to make sure that we are not so busy being clever, and impressing others with how much we know, that we forget to be kind.

Buddhist teachers often say that if we find it hard to understand or put into practice the other Buddhist principles at first, the least thing we can do is be kind to others. This creates the karma for us to be able to understand the rest of Buddha's teachings and progress to enlightenment.

One kind smile is worth a hundred words.

FACE OF AMITAYUS

Amitayus is the red Bodhisattva of "infinite life" or longevity. He sits in meditation posture holding a golden flask full of the nectar of immortality. Its jeweled top appears in the bottom of the illustration.

letting go

Letting go of our attachment to objects and experiences we like, and our aversion to things that we don't care for, is one of the fundamental Buddhist teachings, called renunciation.

Renunciation means being able to let go of our feelings of attachment and aversion, and accept that all things, both pleasant and unpleasant, will always arise and pass in our lives. Impermanence is a simple fact of life. Once you are able to let go of this attachment and aversion, you are better equipped to deal with your emotions when the good things in life pass you by and the awful

PADMAPANI AVALOKITESHVARA

Detail of offerings placed before Padmapani's lotus throne.
The fan-shaped design at the bottom center is inscribed with
the syllables of his mantra, Om–Mani–Padme–Hum.

things come your way. Letting go stops you from creating the bad karma that arises from craving and desire, aversion and hatred.

Clear the mind

Obsessive thoughts can be troubling for days, even causing sleepless nights. A thought may go around and around in the mind, repeating itself time and time again. Usually there is no real resolution until the obsessive thought fades of its own accord.

However, instead of trying to escape from the obsessive thought, learn to embrace and examine it. Then you may conclude that it is, after all, just a thought. It doesn't have to rule the mind, and take away your inner peace. Remind yourself that, however persistent it is, it is still just a thought, then it is easier to let it go.

Accepting yourself as you are

It is easy for people to become obsessed about their bodies, as you can see from the many people who suffer from various eating disorders in our contemporary world. Reflect that very few people can look like fashion models, whose images are presented as the ideal way to look. They are

artificial creations, purely designed to sell clothes. So let go of being dissatisfied with how you look. You are fine the way you are right now.

From the perspective of many lifetimes, or even the immensity of one life, holding onto anything is pointless. All things arise and pass, so let them go easily when their time is up. This creates space for new things to arise in your life.

When you sit in meditation, quietly watching your breath, you will find that thoughts may come thick and fast. Take each one, say to yourself: "This is just a thought," and watch it pass.

THE MAHASIDDHA DARIKAPA

Darikapa, a courtesan's slave, was one of the eighty-four Indian Buddhist Mahasiddhas. He is depicted gazing into a mirror as he plucks his mustache.

Try to create space in your mind
by telling yourself that
repeating these thoughts is not helpful,
that you are making the situation
more intense.
Just let them go!

Martine Batchelor

THE MEDICINE BUDDHA

Bhaisajyaguru, the "Medicine Guru," is the deep blue Buddha of
healing who revealed the Buddhist Medical Tantras. He holds the
attribute of a stem of myrobalan, the medicinal "cherry-plum."

I was angry with my friend,

I told my wrath,

my wrath did end;

I was angry with my foe,

I told it not,

my wrath did grow.

William Blake

THE MAHASIDDHA KHADGAPA

The Mahasiddha Khadgapa, the "sword-holder," holds a wisdom
sword above his head as he transmutes his body into the
elements of water, fire, and air.

Unconditional love

When we fall in love, we create an ideal fiction about our newfound friend. The person seems wonderful in every way. However, experience tells us that after some time we will start to notice faults in our friend, and we will realize that he or she is not as perfect as we first thought. If we let go of the fiction of perfection in our new lover, we can avoid feeling disappointed later on.

The Buddha likened anger to picking up hot coals with your bare hands and throwing them at someone. Both people get hurt, but you get hurt first, and experience the pain of anger inside yourself. The wise person lets go of anger as soon as it arises.

A tightly closed fist tries to grasp hold of things, but they slip away because of the grasping.

Opening yourself to life means you are able to appreciate life as it happens, and then you can let it go naturally as it flows by, without trying to hold it back.

A great Buddhist teacher had a beautiful vase in his room. Everyone who visited him admired this exquisite vase. One day a student came to visit him and opened the door clumsily. The vase fell to the floor and smashed to pieces. The horrified student started to apologize, but noticed that her teacher was smiling and didn't seem upset that his beautiful vase was broken. The student asked her teacher why he didn't mind losing his precious vase. The teacher replied: "I always told myself the vase was already broken, so when one day it did inevitably break I would not feel its loss. You too can learn to let go of your precious possessions in this way."

Letting things go is liberating.
It frees you to get on with living life.

VASUDHARA

Detail of a painting of the golden wealth goddess Vasudhara, showing her right foot, which rests upon a white conch shell and a treasure vase.

Imagine that your mind is like a calm,
clear lake or a vast empty sky:
ripples appear on the surface of the lake
and clouds pass across the sky,
but they soon disappear
without altering the natural stillness.
Thoughts come and go;
they are transient, momentary.
Notice them and let them go, returning your
attention again and again to the breath.

Kathleen McDonald

REFLECTED MOUNTAINS

Detail from a painting of the Mahasiddha Tilopa showing
mountains reflected in a tranquil lake.

There are subtle aspects to letting go, especially in relation to the identity we have created for ourselves. If we perceive ourselves as clever, good, and worthwhile, we must let go of our arrogance, not our feeling of self-worth. If we regard ourselves as stupid and not worth bothering about, we need to let go of our negative self-image, and cultivate a feeling of self-regard.

Look outwardly

The hardest element for anyone to let go of is a sense of their own self-importance. We are often

THE MAHASIDDHA NAGABODHI

Nagabodhi, a jewel thief, was told by his guru to visualize a red horn arising from his head as he meditated in his jewel-filled hut. Eventually he saw the emptiness of the horn and of his own avarice.

guilty of taking ourselves far too seriously, and regarding ourselves as more important than anyone else.

There is a useful Buddhist practice, called "exchanging oneself for others," which helps us to let go of this sense of self-importance. This involves thinking of other people as being as precious as ourselves, and treating them as we would treat ourselves. This creates good karma and helps us let go of the vanity of the self.

Trying to let go is hard;

letting go is easy.

Forgive and forget

When someone does something horrible to you, it is most unpleasant. However, it is important that you let go of that person's negative action toward you as soon as you possibly can. Otherwise, you will simply prolong your own suffering. Try to remember that people who behave badly toward others are only creating the causes to suffer themselves sometime in the future; this should make it easier for you to let go of holding a grudge against them.

A wise Buddhist master was known to have virtually no possessions and was very happy. Many students and other Buddhist teachers would visit the wise old master to hear him teach. But his greatest teaching was giving everything away. When his visitors arrived bearing gifts, he would accept them and promptly give them a gift he had been given previously. Often the next visitor would arrive while the first visitor was still there. Then the first visitor would witness the master giving their precious gift away to the new visitor.

This wonderful teaching allowed people to see the unimportance of possessions, the importance of generosity, and the way to let go of trying to control events.

Put away your beliefs

When we are children, we live life through our pure experience; this is how we learn. But when we grow older, we impose a veil of beliefs and views between ourselves and our experiences, so that we no longer learn so much from them. When we are closed like this, it is much easier to create negative karma. Try letting go of your beliefs, values, and views once in a while, and being truly open to what your experiences can teach you.

Letting go of self-indulgence is a very good form of renunciation. This may seem like a tough thing to change, but try to reduce your habitual indulgences, whether they are food, drink, sex, shopping, or anything else, and you will notice that when you do indulge yourself, you will enjoy the experience them even more. You will also find that you don't crave these things so much if you aren't continually indulging in them. The karmic consequences of craving are then reduced quite substantially as well.

Thinking about letting something go
is not the same as actually doing it.

THE MAHASIDDHA CAPARIPA

Caparipa, the "petrifying guru," is shown in sexual union as "speed-walks" through the sky, bearing his consort over a precipitous gorge.

It's easy to see that we should let go of our bad habits altogether, but we also need to let go of our attachment to good habits.

Here today, gone tomorrow

Life in the present moment can pass us by, while we think nostalgically about the past and fantasize about the future. Let go of dwelling in the past and future, and wake up to your life in the here and now.

The stress of modern life can be tiring, which can develop into anger and depression, if you don't make enough time to be quiet, relax, and meditate. Tiredness can make you irritable with others and thereby unwittingly create negative karma. By letting go of doing too much, you can skillfully free yourself from creating bad karma, and improve the quality of your life.

If you practice letting go as much as possible during your lifetime, not only will you create positive karma for a better rebirth, but at death you will also be able to let go of life itself a little more easily.

Let go into the spaciousness
of simply being.

Acknowledge each feeling
(as it arises), and then let it go.
If you do not continue with it,
then you will be free of that feeling.
Similar thoughts and feelings
may come again,
but just treat them the same.

Diana St. Ruth

CLOUDS

Detail of billowing cumulus clouds, from a painting
of Shakyamuni Buddha.

a good
life

No killing and no stealing,

no abusing and no lying,

no slandering, swearing, gossiping,

no coveting, resenting, or fixating:

these pristine acts are ways to practice

that ripen as beauty and pleasure

here and elsewhere.

Nagarjuna

WISH FULFILLING TREE

Detail of the Wish Fulfilling Tree showing birds, flowers,
silks, and jewels.

The present life is the result of
the past karmic activity,
and the future life is the result of
the present life activity.

Nyanatiloka Mahathera

WHITE TARA

The three eyes in White Tara's face represent the purity of her
body, speech, and mind; the eyes in her palms and soles represent
the four immeasurables of love, compassion, joy, and equanimity.

I n Buddhism, our existence is referred to as "this precious human life." People in the West, by and large, have sound minds and bodies, a place to live, enough food to eat, clean water to drink, and medicine when sick.

However, there are people living in our world today who are not so fortunate. According to the law of karma, we personally created the causes for our present comfortable existence in our previous lives and also were fortunate enough to meet the right conditions for the positive karma to ripen in this current life. Therefore it is important for us to continue being kind, wise, and generous, in order to create the conditions for our next lives to be good ones too.

If we just waste our time using up our good karma and creating negative karma, our next life will not be so pleasant.

A good life
is not dependent on wealth
and possessions.

Most of the truly good things in life, such as happiness, contentment, and inner peace, come from inside us. If your mind is tranquil, and you have equanimity in the face of good fortune and bad fortune alike, then your well-being is not easily disturbed.

Do not be envious of those you see around you who have good lives. Instead, you should work to create the positive karma that will bring the good things in life to you.

How can we live happily when we see others who are less fortunate? Helping others as much as we can not only increases our positive karma to experience a good life in the future, but also creates feelings of satisfaction now, which arise as a result of our being kind and helpful to others.

Witnessing the happiness of others helps us enjoy our own good life.

Simply refraining from negative
and unskillful actions that create
bad karma is both living well
and creating the causes for this
good life to continue.

Cultivating awareness

Living with awareness helps us make the most of a good life. If we daydream and have fantasies about living a different kind of life, or some unattainable ideal existence, then we will use up the good karma of our current good life. Instead of arriving in the future kind of paradise we dreamed about, we will not gain another precious human rebirth, because we did not create the causes for it while we had the opportunity.

What is a good life?

A good life is living with kindness, generosity, and other virtues, and thereby finding happiness for oneself through these actions.

CRANES IN A LANDSCAPE

Detail of a painting of Manjushri showing a pair of cranes,
which symbolize longevity, harmony, and fidelity.

If we greet situations with a positive attitude, we will eventually create positive returns. If we respond with a negative attitude, negative things will eventually come our way.

Tenzin Palmo

A DELUGE

Detail of a painting of the Mahasiddha Ghantapa, depicting a flood engulfing the palace of the king.

Selfishness only makes us miserable; it creates a mentality of meanness, which prevents us finding real happiness. If we look carefully at selfish people, we can see they are even mean to themselves at times. They are so concerned about making sure no one else shares what they have that it becomes a major preoccupation. This causes them suffering. Consequently, they are unable to find happiness in this life, and they create the karma which will enable them to experience more suffering in future lives.

Karma affects past and future lives, but if you find this a difficult idea, you can think about it in terms of just this current life. As the result of living a good life in the past, you have been blessed with a human life and are relatively fortunate. Understanding that living a good life now creates the karma for fortunate circumstances later can bring you inner peace.

Even during the life span of one fortunate rebirth, we will encounter problems. The very nature of our existence involves dissatisfaction and suffering. This is called "samsara," the cycle of birth and rebirth that only finishes when we finally attain Buddhahood. If we can practice equanimity equally in the face of good and bad fortune, then we keep our peace of mind, and are less likely to act in a manner that will cause future suffering.

A good life is lived in harmony with Nature.

The middle way

Following the Buddha's "middle way" approach helps us live a good life. The "middle way" is a path that avoids extremes, which helps us avoid the suffering that comes from excess. This is quite easy to see in our lives. For example, if we eat too much or too little, we experience either indigestion or hunger. If either extreme becomes a habit, then our health suffers, and we might die early of a heart attack or malnutrition. Eating moderate amounts of healthy food creates one of the causes for a good life in this lifetime.

Live life as if each day were the last. In this way, you will make the most of each and every day, and enjoy a good life.

Finding a balance between meaningful activity and time for meditation and other relaxing activities will help you find the satisfaction that leads to inner peace.

Regardless of what we believe,
our actions will reverberate
beyond our deaths.

Stephen Batchelor

MANDALA DESIGN

Detail of a visionary painting of Four-armed Avalokiteshvara,
showing a corner of its intricate mandala design.

You may find the idea of rebirth rather difficult to grasp or understand. After all, it is difficult to prove that rebirth actually happens, and our Western scientific minds like empirical evidence. However, you can simply focus on living a good life here and now, both for your own well-being and because you know the results of your actions will outlive you. For example, giving some money to support the digging and maintenance of a well in a developing country in the Third World will have a powerful beneficial effect on many people's lives in the present, and also for a long time after your death.

Living well is the best revenge.

Proverb

Although Buddhism does not advocate taking revenge on other people because, from the point of view of karma, it can harm both receiver and perpetrator, this proverb has an underlying, more subtle meaning. Living well after someone has wronged us is the best way to get on with living our lives. This is not really revenge at all, and, in fact, is better than any form of revenge that harms another.

A kind heart is the sign of a good life.

It's easy to smile

when life flows along

like a happy song,

But the one who's worthwhile

is the one with a smile

When everything goes quite wrong.

Traditional song

LANDSCAPE

Detail of a painting of Thousand-armed Avalokiteshvara, showing
clouds, rocks, and a lake, and jewels, leaves, and lotuses.

If you've lived a good life and suddenly then encounter bad fortune, don't feel that you have lived your earlier life in a wrong way. Karma works on many levels, over many different lifetimes.

The misfortune you suffer now is negative karma ripening from causes in a previous life. Experiencing it now means that you won't have to suffer it later. You may not be able to transform the misfortune into something more positive, but you can transform your feelings about it by seeing it from the perspective of karma.

Once upon a time in ancient Tibet, a Buddhist monk took the teachings on karma very seriously.

He realized that his good karma had produced a precious human life fortunate enough to ensure that he encountered the Buddha's teachings, but that it would one day be exhausted. So he decided to make sure that he did more positive deeds than negative ones in order to create merit. Each night he sat before a pile of stones and recalled his every action and thought during the day. For each good one, he placed a stone on the right; for each bad one, he put a stone on the left. Every night he saw how much positive and negative karma he had created that day. This encouraged him to lead as good a life as possible.

From here to eternity

When we are old and near death, we look back over our lives. If we have lived a bad life, we will feel full of regret, and we will die unhappy. If we heard about karma and still lived a bad life, we will feel fearful of what will come in future lives. But if we lived a good life, we will feel only happy, with no regrets, and no fear of whatever lies in store for us in another existence.

A good life is not one enormous thing that you get either right or wrong. It is composed of lots of little acts of kindness and wisdom.

THE MAHASIDDHA TANTEPA

Tantepa was a gambler who utilized the game of dice as a method of meditation. He holds a dice in his right hand and a skull-cup of alcohol in his left hand.

Someone who is not critical of others, either to their faces or behind their backs, is a person who is trying to live a good life.

The great sages from all religions lived lives of humility and simplicity. This is a good way of living that we can aspire to, until we reach the point where we no longer believe that worldly and material treasures are a source of happiness.

The wise know that a good life depends on the inner treasures of virtue and wisdom, because only these will create positive karma, leading eventually to the state of Buddhahood where karma is finished altogether.

One good life begets another. But how do we live a good life? The first thing to do is to refrain from harming others or yourself. The second is to start actively being of benefit to others.

Look at the people in this world who live truly good lives. They are setting a wonderful example that you can try to emulate. Rejoice that you too can live a good life from this moment on.

Perhaps the essence of a good life is to have genuine concern for others as much as, or even more than, for yourself. This brings peace and happiness to yourself and those around you in this life, while creating positive karma for future lives.

The most sublime act is
to set another before you.

William Blake

faith

It is perhaps quite true
that a direct proof for rebirth
cannot be given.

Nyanatiloka Mahathera

LOTUS

Detail of a lotus blossom arising from a lake.

There are many things we have to take on trust in life, and many things that carry no guarantees. In the spiritual sphere, trust develops into an art form that we work with creatively; this is faith. The Buddhist teachings encourage us to investigate everything for ourselves, and not to blindly accept things just because someone has said they are true.

True faith is not blind trust, but neither does someone with faith have irrefutable proof of anything. It is most important to develop faith that the Buddha's teachings, such as those of karma and rebirth, will help us find happiness and avoid suffering, and eventually lead us to enlightenment.

True faith

Believing that the law of karma is true and correct is a relief; it means we can trust that causes have effects that will eventually come to pass. Faith in the workings of karma leads us toward inner peace, because it lessens our concerns about whether natural justice occurs.

If one of your aims is to deepen your faith in karma, you should think as much as possible about how karma operates, and remember that every action of body, speech, and mind causes an ultimate effect.

> Faith in the workings of karma
> helps us to take responsibility
> for our actions.

Your faith in karma can be seriously challenged when you see someone act really badly and then appear to benefit from the negative behavior. But you cannot see the whole picture. A person who does something that hurts someone else has sown seeds of bad karma that will definitely ripen when the right circumstances arise. This often happens in another lifetime, but sometimes you also see bad people receive their karmic comeuppance in the same life.

Three great qualities

The Zen tradition speaks of three things that need to be cultivated on the Buddhist path:

Great Faith,

Great Doubt,

and Great Courage.

We can be very nice people
but still have lots of problems.
On the other hand, we can be awful
people and have a wonderful time.
But from a Buddhist perspective,
it's just a matter of time
before we receive the results
of our conduct.

Tenzin Palmo

DRAGON AND TIGER

The earthly tiger and heavenly dragon are Chinese symbols of
yin and yang. The background landscape depicts Mount Kailas
and Lake Manasarovar in western Tibet.

These three qualities keep our spiritual inquiry alive, so that we do not take life for granted. Faith, doubt, and courage help us see that we really know nothing. With this attitude, often referred to as Beginner's Mind, we are no longer hemmed in by our beliefs. We can open our hearts and minds to new levels of understanding.

When we feel weak,

faith gives us strength.

In whom or what should we have faith? We need faith that following the Buddha's path will free us from suffering, and we need faith in ourselves to carry on walking that path, even when we are tired and discouraged.

A test of faith

By developing faith in karma, you will start to see how it works in your own life. When you see karma operating in your life and the lives of others, your faith in karma strengthens.

Putting your faith in karma
does not absolve you from the
consequences of your own actions.

Faith is not equivalent to mere belief.
Faith is the condition of
ultimate confidence that we have
the capacity to follow
the path of doubt to its end.

Stephen Batchelor

KALACHAKRA MANDALA LANDSCAPE

Detail of a painting of White Padmapani, depicting lotuses,
leaves, water, cliffs, and distant cloud-capped mountains.

How can we have true faith and belief in karma when we cannot scientifically prove that karma actually exists? Embrace the concept of karma, but keep questioning it until your faith is able to arise naturally.

A personal mission

When your faith in karma is strong, you feel less disappointed when life doesn't go your way. If someone acts unpleasantly toward you, you know that person will suffer the effects of the bad karma. You also know that if you let it go and do

THE DAKINI THROMA NAGMO

Throma Nagmo, the "wrathful black goddess," is a wrathful manifestation of the goddess Vajra Yogini. Her practice is employed in the Chod ritual for severing attachments.

not act badly in response, then you are not creating further bad karma for yourself. Having faith and understanding in the law of karma helps you live with peace and calm, rather than feeling you have to respond to everything that comes your way.

Even if you feel you are not clever and don't know much, you can still develop faith in karma. Faith does not depend on being clever.

Having faith in karma
will reap its own rewards
in the fullness of time.

When you have faith in karma, you can no longer blame your unpleasant experiences on bad luck. Understanding that you created the causes for such experiences through previous negative actions, which have now met conducive conditions for the karma to ripen, may be difficult, but it gives you a sense of having some control over your destiny. This inspires you to act with good intentions, and brings you peace of mind.

Faith is felt in the
depths of the heart,
not the ripples of the mind.

You are always creating karma

During the course of each day, remind yourself from time to time that all of your thoughts, words, and actions are creating karma, and that it is best to avoid creating negative karmic consequences for yourself. Concentrate on behaving in ways that will bring peace and happiness to you now and in the future.

Try to think before you act. If your faith in karma is strong, it will guide you toward positive, wholesome actions, and away from actions that will cause you future suffering.

PADMAPANI AVALOKITESHVARA

The white bodhisattva of compassion and "holder of the lotus" (Padmapani).

Essentially, you should always have faith
that your own physical, verbal, and
mental states, and all your different
impulses, arise from the Buddha's
physical, verbal, and mental states,
and all his different impulses.

Li T'ung Hsuan

CLOUDS

Detail of swirling clouds in a dark blue sky from a painting
of White Tara.

If you have faith that
ultimately you too
can become a Buddha,
this will strengthen your determination
to follow the spiritual path.

You must keep questioning if your faith is not to be blind. Do not let go of your own inquiring mind in the quest to develop faith. The Buddha's "middle way" lies between the extremes of blind faith and intransigent reason, and is a good approach to the teachings on karma.

Wishing everyone happiness

Our faith in the law of karma should develop our wish for everyone, not just ourselves, to enjoy the results of good karma, and not to suffer the effects of bad karma. We can skillfully encourage the people around us to refrain from negative actions, and to engage in wholesome activity.

Our faith in karma may or may not include fully believing in rebirth. If we find rebirth over-whelming or difficult at first, then it is helpful to look at how karma operates over one lifetime. In this case, we refrain from negative actions in order to find peace and happiness in the present life.

But if there is no other world
and there is no fruit
and ripening of actions
well done or ill done,
then here and now in this life
I shall be free from
hostility, affliction, and anxiety,
and I shall live happily.

Buddha

LEAVES AND FRUIT

Detail of a painting of the Mahasiddha Jalandhara showing
clusters of leaves, which bear three fruits as symbols of the
Buddha, dharma, and Sangha.

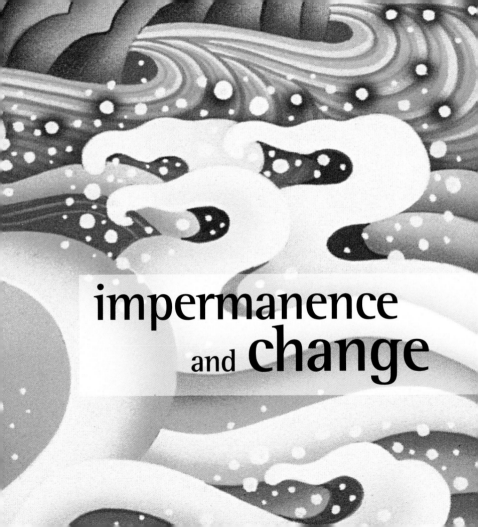

impermanence
and change

All life is a flowing,
a continual process of becoming,
change and transformation.

Nyanatiloka Mahathera

WATERFALL

Detail of a painting of the Mahasiddha Kantalipa, showing a
waterfall cascading through a rocky landscape.

When we create karma through our actions, speech, and thoughts, it generates effects that will be experienced at a future point. However, after we experience the full results of any karma we have created, it is exhausted and the effect of the original karmic act is finished. All karmic results are impermanent. How we respond to these results is then what becomes important.

Consider the case of an habitual thief. His thefts might cause the karmic consequence of his house burning down so that he loses everything. If he responds to this misfortune by continuing to steal, he will generate further bad karma for himself.

However, if the thief's tragedy makes him realize the error of his ways, and he resolves never to steal again, then he will not create further bad karma, and he will have learned the karmic lesson.

Realizing that all things are impermanent is crucial to understanding how karma works. Once you know that all things are impermanent, it becomes much easier to be less attached to your possessions and relationships. Your desire and craving then become less extreme, and you will generate less negative karma as a result.

We live our lives unconsciously believing that things will be permanent, until we are faced with

the loss or breakage of something, such as losing our car keys or breaking our arm. It is only when we temporarily lose the use of our broken arm or are unable to drive a car because of losing the keys that we realize their respective values.

It is only then that we realize these things are impermanent. We can practice not taking things for granted, consciously appreciating the value of everything we encounter and use in our lives.

Life itself is impermanent and will be transformed into death.

CLOUDS

Detail of a gold-on-black painting of the wrathful deity Mahamaya, showing clouds and a section of his fiery aura.

All actions take place in time by the
interweaving of the forces of Nature,
but the man lost in selfish delusion
thinks that he himself is the actor.

The Bhagavad Gita

Each of us is just one of an infinite number of beings passing through the present moment, experiencing the results of our karma.

Our lives are intermingled with the lives of others and with our environment, so we live and act interdependently with others and Nature. We do not operate in a void.

Thus, the idea that we are the principal actor in our lives is actually a delusion; we are simply part of the ongoing pattern of life, forever in flux and forever in change.

What we experience and how we experience it is due to our karma. All phenomena arise in dependence on causes and conditions. This means that when the conditions that brought something into existence in the first place inevitably change, then the thing itself must also change, and is revealed as impermanent.

Change permeates our existence, causing suffering and dissatisfaction. For example, on a hot, sunny day you may enjoy lying in the sun, but after a while it becomes too hot and it is a relief to jump into a cool lake and swim around. However, after some time, you feel cold and tired so that you need to change your situation by getting out of the lake and into the sun again.

It is as if things and events carry
the seed of their own eventual demise.
The simple reason is that anything
that is produced through causes
is other-powered: its very existence
comes about only in dependence
upon other factors.

The Dalai Lama

EIGHT AUSPICIOUS SYMBOLS

Detail of a painting of the Eight Auspicious Buddhist Symbols,
showing the golden vase, lotus, and eternal knot, and a part of
the two golden fishes and victorious banner.

Watch a sunflower as the sun sinks in the evening, and observe how the flower turns and shuts. In the morning, the flower turns toward the sun and opens. Observing the ever-changing cycles of Nature is a good meditation to remind ourselves that all things are impermanent and will change.

Positive karma, positive change

Meditating upon impermanence and suffering helps us strengthen our wish to be free from suffering. To be free from suffering, we must

GREEN TARA

Detail of a copy of an early Nepali painting of the goddess Green Tara, showing her ornate jewelry and her left hand holding a blue lotus.

cease creating the causes of suffering. We should try to cultivate only skillful, wholesome behavior in order to create positive karma. Impermanence is liberating because it carries the potential for people to change for the better.

Bad habits cause repeated cycles of negative karma. Reflect that each moment contains the seed for change. If you are willing to try hard enough, you can change any aspect of yourself, including breaking free from your bad habits.

Look for the causes of your unskillful actions and try to change them. For example, if you habitually get angry, make a point of not expressing the anger the next time it arises. Instead, go somewhere quiet and look at the causes underlying the anger. This might be frustration, a sense of impotence, or pure rage. Realize the feeling will pass and it is not worth exacerbating a situation by expressing anger. Try to feel compassion for yourself, and determine to let go of the intensity of the anger.

Although nice things give us pleasure, because they are impermanent they pass and we experience suffering after they are gone. It's important to notice this in your own life. Think of all the pleasurable experiences you've had. Did any of them last? Perhaps the experience did not go away, but your reaction to it changed into boredom or irritation.

Whatever happened was characterized by change and dissatisfaction; there is nothing that can give lasting satisfaction.

The concept of linear time is a misleading idea; we can only exist in the present moment, here and now. The past is gone forever; the future never arrives. The present moment is forever changing, as is everything in it, including ourselves. Relax into the moment; it is all that we have, and it is gone before we realize it.

The realization that you can change your negative behavior and thereby no longer create so much bad karma for yourself will bring you a sense of relief. It may be hard work, but you will find inner peace when you succeed.

When you meditate, you observe how your mind is constantly changing. Thoughts arise, then they pass and are replaced by other thoughts. Your feelings change all the time too; one minute you are depressed, then something nice happens and you feel happy. Investing in thoughts or feelings, believing they have real substance, only causes suffering, because they are changing all the time.

Who am I,
Standing in the midst of this
Thought-traffic?

Jalaluddin Rumi

THOUSAND-ARMED AVALOKITESHVARA

Avalokiteshvara, the Bodhisattva of compassion, is depicted
here in his eleven-headed form with a thousand hands and a
thousand eyes. To his lower right and left are his two attendant
Bodhisattvas, Sadaksari and Manidhara.

If you meditate frequently on impermanence, gradually you will come to expect change as an integral part of life, and accept it gracefully.

No one can avoid change; it occurs all the time. But you don't have to feel powerless, because you can initiate change in yourself.

You can live life
more happily by
choosing to change
for the better.

CLOUDS

Detail of a painting of Red Avalokiteshvara, showing a bank of cumulus clouds.

The world changes every moment in subtle ways. Every time you blink, some change has happened somewhere that will have an indirect or direct effect on your life.

Nothing is so bad
that it cannot change.

Our precious self is also impermanent and will die. But are we exactly the same self from moment to moment?

Buddhist teachings suggest that the self has no real existence, that if we try to pinpoint where exactly the self is, we cannot. We can't say that our self is our heart, our mind, or anything else. Do we actually exist beyond the thoughts flowing through our minds?

Because we can change ourselves, we can also change our karma. In this way, we are responsible for creating our own happiness or suffering, inner turmoil or inner peace.

One of the fundamental and most important teachings of the Buddha is that all phenomena are impermanent. So, do not cling to those things that will change because it will only cause suffering in the future.

When I consider everything that grows

Holds in perfection but a little moment,

That this huge stage presenteth naught but shows

Whereon the stars in secret influence comment . . .

Then the conceit of this inconstant stay

Sets you most rich in youth before my sight,

Where wasteful Time debateth with Decay,

To change your day of youth to sullied night . . .

William Shakespeare

THE NIGHT SKY

Detail of a painting of the Mahasiddha Acinta, showing the
silhouettes of rocks against the stars of the night sky.

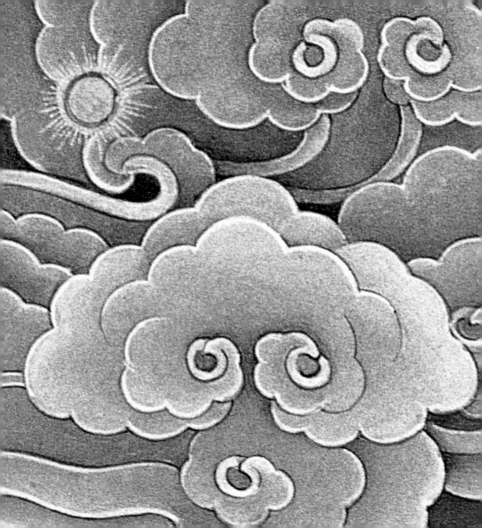

regret and
resolve

There is no saint
without a past
and no sinner
without a future.

Babaji

THE WEALTH GOD JAMBHALA

The wealth deity Yellow Jambhala, holding the attributes of a
citron fruit in his right hand, and a jewel-disgorging mongoose
in his left hand.

The act of willingly recalling our past actions is the first step toward regretting our unskillful behavior and resolving not to act in this manner again. If we have done something we know is wrong or hurtful, usually we are tempted to forget our action as quickly as possible. However, we cannot forgo the karmic fruit of our negative actions by forgetting about them.

When we meditate, old memories
tend to surface in the mind.
This is an ideal opportunity
to assess our behavior.

If you remember shouting angrily at a friend, you can reflect upon how much you hurt him or her. You will feel genuine sorrow and regret for your unskillful action. You can then resolve to try not to shout angrily at people again.

How to stop behaving badly
Regretting past negative actions helps create the karma for not repeating them.

When you consciously resolve to stop behaving badly, you sow the seeds of positive karma in the unconscious mind. Then, when circumstances tempt you to respond in your old bad ways, a little voice in the back of your mind reminds you of your resolution. Listen to it!

Peace begins in our own
hearts when we are willing to
acknowledge our wrong deeds and
make the resolution
to live in harmony with others.

Recollect and reflect

Before you can develop sincere regret, you must first make an effort to recollect actions that are considered unwholesome. Then reflect upon them until you realize that they have created negative karmic imprints that will cause you future suffering. This will strongly motivate you to behave in a better manner in the future, and to resolve not to repeat such negative actions again.

If you hurt someone really badly, you are haunted by the ghost of that action. The person's pained face appears in your mind and even in your dreams, and then you are filled with remorse. This is a karmic consequence of an unwholesome action that lurks in your unconscious mind until you do something to change it. Bringing the action to mind, meditating on its painful impact, and then experiencing deep regret helps to exorcise the memory, and to exhaust the karmic consequence.

You should not be frightened of making mistakes on your journey through life, as this is a natural part of being human. But you do need to regret your mistaken actions, by understanding what caused them, and to accept that there will be a negative karmic result. Then you can learn from your mistakes and resolve not to make them again. In this way, you gradually learn to transform all of your negative actions of body, speech, and mind into positive ones, which eventually will lead to inner peace.

If you think before you act, and realize that one of the consequences of your action will be regret, you will see it is better not to act in the first place.

A wrong action regretted,

together with the resolve

not to repeat it,

is a lesson well learned.

Ask yourself this: "Do I want to keep on creating bad karma from all my negative actions, and experiencing the suffering as a result?" Of course you don't! So practice regretting negative actions and resolving not to act in this manner again.

Avoiding suffering

Do not push away feelings of regret, even if they are painful. The power of regret can help you transform your life, but if you do not regret your bad actions, you are likely to repeat them, which will keep you trapped in a cycle of suffering.

It is important not to confuse regret with guilt. Guilt is a negative emotion involving fear and

BURNING INCENSE IN A LANDSCAPE

Detail of a painting of Green Tara, showing an offering of incense burning beneath her lotus throne.

anxiety, but regret is a thoughtful and honest response to any negative actions we may have committed, and is, therefore, a positive emotion.

Reforming our character

Sincere regret for adverse actions leads to the natural resolve not to repeat such unskillful behavior again. This in turn leads naturally to reforming one's character and disposition, so the ability to behave skillfully becomes spontaneous.

We need to be realistic when we resolve not to repeat negative actions. Though we may genuinely not want to fall into our old negative behavioral patterns again, it is likely that we will fall by the wayside from time to time. This is simply because we are human. We are likely to fail completely, however, if we set ourselves such a momentous task as never, ever to be angry again.

Then, when we find ourselves in a rage and recall our resolve, we feel weak and a failure, and stop trying to avoid negative actions altogether because we feel it is impossible to do so. This is counterproductive. The best way forward is to start by resolving not to be angry for an hour, then a morning, then a whole day. This is using resolve in a more realistic and effective way.

One who previously made bad kamma,
but who reforms
and creates good kamma,
brightens the world like the moon
appearing from behind a cloud.

Dhammapada

MOON, CLOUDS, AND AURA

Detail of a painting of Vajrasattva, showing clouds, part of his
aura, the radiant crescent moon, and the "lucky constellation"
of the Pleiades.

One way to avoid regret caused by unskillful actions is to try consciously to be skillful from moment to moment throughout the day. This includes practicing positive actions such as kindness.

Positive states of mind are beneficial and lead to positive action, thereby creating good karma and happiness. Negative states of mind are harmful to ourselves and others and lead to bad karma and regret.

Negative states of mind such as anger, desire, and hatred are not inherently evil; they are simply negative mental energy. There is no need to feel ashamed when they arise in us because it is natural to have such feelings from time to time. If you respond to these emotions by analyzing them and observing how they lead only to suffering and regret, it is easier to resolve not to act out the feeling in a way that will create negative karma. Sincere regret can only arise in the mind when we truly understand the impact and consequences of an unskillful action.

We can regret not performing good actions, as well as performing bad actions.

Regret cannot undo an unskillful action, but it can lead to the resolve not to repeat it.

So it can be very beneficial from time to time to think back over our lives, starting from when we were young, and calling to mind the mistakes we have made. If we do this we will discover many things of which we usually remain unaware. If we then generate sincere regret and concentrate our meditation on purifying those particular [karmic] imprints, we shall be effectively able to eliminate the obstacles which would otherwise arise as a result of them.

Geshe Rabten

FLOWERS AND AURA

Detail of a painting of a Bodhisattva, showing lotus flowers and leaves within the aura.

Reflect, then regret, but do not forget your actions that have caused suffering.

Meditation III

Take five minutes to meditate. Calm the mind by watching your breath enter and leave your body. Now resolve not to create any negative actions of body, speech, or mind for the next hour. Make a promise to yourself that you will really try hard. Then meditate again when the hour is up and observe how your mind feels.

GREEN TARA

The goddess of mercy and compassion, who holds an utapala lotus flower.

The road to hell is paved with good intentions.

If we look at this old proverb, we see that good intentions are wonderful, but not always easy to live up to. So do not be too hard on yourself if you cannot fulfill your resolve to act skillfully all of the time. Self-criticism leads to the hell of self-doubt, and you might become so discouraged that you abandon the idea of behaving well altogether.

We've all done horrible things, but it is important not to worry. We do some purification, feel regret, and do our best not to do such things any more.

FLAMES AND CLOUDS

Detail of a painting of the wrathful deity Hayagriva, showing flames and gold on black clouds.

patience

There is no evil like hatred,
And no fortitude like patience.
Thus I should strive in various ways
To meditate on patience.

Shantideva

Patience is one of the greatest virtues, and practicing patience means our inner peace is not disturbed. In Buddhism, patience is considered one of the six perfections, or ideal qualities, that help lead us toward a happy life, and eventual enlightenment. Being patient means no longer reacting with anger when someone acts hurtfully or aggressively toward us. Instead, we should try to respond with love and compassion, by remembering that the person who is being hurtful must be suffering in order to behave in such an unskillful manner. The angry, aggressive person is creating negative karma, so we feel compassion for him or her, as he or she will experience the karmic fruits of the negative action in the future.

If you behave patiently when things go wrong, you are less likely to behave in unskillful ways and create bad karma for yourself.

Cultivating a patient attitude
brings inner peace and
creates good karma.

Patience is being able to forgive someone who has hurt us immediately, without holding a grudge against him or her.

We often think that it is impossible
to develop perfect patience; however,
if we know our nature and our qualities,
and if we train ourselves in them,
it is completely possible to do it.

Bokar Rinpoche

FLOWERS, RAINBOW, AND ROCKS

Detail of a painting of Four-armed Avalokiteshvara, showing
part of his rainbow aura with rocks and lotus flowers.

Peace of mind

Being patient with ourselves and others helps prevent negative states of mind from arising. This helps us to avoid bad behavior—caused by feeling angry, irritated, and so forth—which creates bad karma. Through practicing patience, we create the causes to help us maintain peace of mind, and to live a joyful life.

Hatred and anger are our greatest enemies. They make us lose our peace of mind, as well as create bad karma as we act out our anger and hatred.

Patience is one of the best antidotes to counteract hatred and anger when they arise.

Tolerance is an aspect of patience that helps us keep calm when we are faced with difficult circumstances.

Suffering and dissatisfaction pervade life and are inescapable. You can't prevent unsatisfactory circumstances from arising. However, you can learn how to deal with difficult situations. If you practice patience in the face of adversity, not only do you keep your peace of mind, but you don't behave unskillfully and create negative karma.

If someone shouts angrily at us, we tend to feel angry in response. If we behave angrily too, the situation is aggravated, because there are now two angry people. If we realize we don't have to behave in this way, and practice patience, the situation will be resolved, since the angry person will calm down if not provoked by our anger.

Dealing with anger

Anger is a very powerful emotion, so how best can you learn to deal with it? If someone speaks viciously to you, you can reflect that their words are just words; they have no enduring quality and will pass quickly if you don't hold on to them. You don't have to respond with anger; you can respond calmly, with patience.

Buddhism teaches us that our enemy is our best friend. This sounds like a contradiction, but if we reflect that our enemy is offering us opportunities to practice patience, which creates positive karma, then in fact it is true, because practicing patience creates the causes of our future happiness.

A patient temperament is more precious than a mountain of money.

Patience can overcome all adversity. So, nurture patience till it takes strong root in your heart.

There is nothing whatsoever that is
not made easier through acquaintance.
So through becoming acquainted with
small harms, I should learn
to patiently accept greater harms.

Shantideva

Detail from a painting of the Mahasiddha Saraha, the "arrow-maker,"
showing an arrow penetrating a tree and arrows in a pot.

Be patient with yourself when you do something silly or wrong and feel irritated with yourself. If you can be patient with yourself, you have a better chance of being patient with others.

Patience can help us deal with many of our problems. If we regard our problems as teachers, providing us with a chance to learn something, then we become less distressed when problems arise. Next time a problematic situation arises, instead of immediately reacting in a negative manner, ask yourself:

What can I learn from this?

Next time you feel angry, practice patience by taking five deep breaths before you say or do anything. Let your mind dwell on the foolishness of an angry response.

The benefits of patience are immeasurable. Try meditating for five minutes on how the strength of patience overcomes anger, the gentleness of patience develops inner peace, and the wisdom of patience helps us act sensibly.

Impatience seems integral to our modern world. We rush around between home, workplace, friends, and activities. If anything delays us, or gets in our way, we become impatient and irritable. Practicing patience in these circumstances maintains our inner peace, so that, when we do arrive where we are going, we can focus on whatever it is we will be doing with a calm mind.

Patience helps us slow down to a healthy pace. Look at the slow rhythm of life in isolated rural communities. People live in harmony with Nature, and this helps them to be naturally patient.

Dealing with impatience

We are so impatient that we tend to rush through our lives trying to cram too much in, afraid we might miss out on something. To counteract impatience, try deliberately missing an habitual activity. Instead, walk somewhere really slowly, and see how calm you feel upon arriving. Doing this regularly helps you develop patience, and transforms your impatience into inner peace.

We can learn about patience by watching a mother helping her child learn to walk. As many times as the child falls, she catches him, steadies him, and lets him try again. Her patience seems boundless. So, when someone is irritating us by repeating a mistake, we can remember our own mothers' patience with us when we were babies, and be patient with the person making mistakes.

The law of karma states that the physical karmic result of practicing patience is an attractive body and demeanor. Consider how this is manifested by observing the pleasant features of a patient person and the ugly, distorted features of someone who is angry.

Patience is our greatest friend

Patience is our greatest friend, as it prevents us from accruing negative karma. Eventually, the practice of patience will help lead us to enlightenment, a state where we are free of karma.

FACE OF VAJRASATTVA

Detail of Vajrasattva, the white Bodhisattva of purification.
He wears golden necklaces, earrings, and a crown of five jewels.

Those people who are patient, even in
difficult circumstances, are esteemed by
all who know them.

TIBETAN LANDSCAPE

Detail of a painting of the dragon and tiger, showing the
landscape of Western Tibet and the monastery of Chiu Gompa.

When the fire of hatred
blazes within our mind,
it is the cool waters of patience
that can put it out.

Geshe Rabten

OFFERINGS UPON A LOTUS

Detail of a painting of White Tara, showing dew-sprinkled lotus
leaves and a red lotus bearing the offerings of a mirror, a lute,
a perfumed conch, burning incense, and jewels.

About the artist

Robert Beer (born 1947), a British artist, has studied and practiced Tibetan thangka painting for more than thirty years. One of the first Westerners to become actively involved in this art form, he initially studied for a period of five years in India and Nepal with several of the finest Tibetan artists living at that time. Since 1975 he has lived in Britain and worked consistently on developing the artistic skills, vision, patience, and understanding of this highly complex subject, as well as the historical and cultural context within which it arises. His drawings and paintings have appeared in several hundred books on Tibetan Buddhist art and religion, and he is widely regarded as one of the world's leading experts on this subject. His publications include *The Encyclopedia of Tibetan Symbols and Motifs* and *The Handbook of Tibetan Buddhist Symbols*.

Over the last ten years he has been commissioning and collecting works by the finest contemporary Nepali and Tibetan artists, and he has been instrumental in introducing the skills of Tibetan art to some of the most accomplished Indian miniature painters of Rajasthan. The paintings of many of these artists appear in this book, and include the Newar artists: Siddhimuni and Surendra Man Shakya, Udaya and Dinesh Charan Shrestha, Lalman Lama, Ajay Lama, Sundar Singhwal, Devendra Singhwal, Samundra Singhwal, Amrit Dangol, Raj Prakash, Amrit Devendra, Kungchang Lama, Ratna Bahadur and Sundar Shrestha. The Tibetan artists include Chewang Lama, Phunsok Tsering, and the studios of Cho Tsering and Dawa-la. The Rajastani artists include Babulal and Jai Shankar, both of whom have worked under the supervision of Marc Baudin of Jaipur.